THE WAR PLAYS

FOUR ONE-ACTS

ANDREW BISS

ENTR'ACTE
EDITIONS

"In war, truth is the first casualty."

— Aeschylus

CONTENTS

An Introduction by the Playwright

While the four plays in this collection range in style from stark realism to heightened reality, they are all unified by one common theme: the Iraq War.

I'm certainly not about to rehash here all of the events that led up to that ignominious period of modern history. That information is freely available elsewhere for anyone who didn't live through it. But I did live through it, and it affected me on such all-consuming, fundamental level that I was compelled to write about it. It was not a choice, but rather a psychological, emotional, and physical compulsion to express how I felt about the harrowing catastrophe that was unfolding around me at the time.

The military tactic of so-called "shock and awe" that was unleashed upon Baghdad at the beginning of the invasion was intended to cow the Iraqis into submission through the use of overwhelming, massive firepower – a sort of modern day blitzkrieg. Sadly, thousands of innocent civilians, many of them women and young children, never survived the onslaught to be either shocked or awed, their words of deference to the military superiority of their attackers forever silenced. But for the outsider looking on, one would have to be a particularly callous, cold-hearted individual not to be, at the very least, "shocked" by those early scenes of carnage. As we saw, collateral damage – that most dehumanizing of military euphemisms – bleeds.

I also lost friends during that war. Not in the conflict itself, thankfully, but socially – people who couldn't understand why I would vehemently decry what I was bearing witness to instead of joining in the chorus of patriotic fervor for a made-up, pointless war destined to bring death and heartache to thousands on both sides. I suppose you could call them my collateral damage. I would sincerely hope, however, that with the benefit of hindsight some of them may have grown from that experience and come to realize that faith, as admirable as it is, is only as good as the person or people with whom you choose to place it in.

Each of these plays approaches the conflict from a different angle. In *Dedication*, I wanted to write a literal dedication to those in the military who gave their lives for a cause that they may or may not have fully understood or believed in. In either instance, their own dedication to duty can only be commended. But the play is also a dedication to the parents of the fallen, who, having lost a beloved son or daughter, must grapple with the question of what exactly that sacrifice was made for – and if it was worth the price.

Degraded is a more expansive view of the invasion of the country itself, employing the metaphor of a battered wife, already ground down by years of abuse and oppression, who must now confront external forces that purport to be her savior but in reality only compound her misery.

The two individuals that I based the husband and wife on in *The Joneses* shouldn't be too hard to figure out, gender aside. Their "special relationship" marks a shift to satire in the third play in the collection, as these modern-day missionaries discover that their sanctimonious meddling has real-life consequences, and that waging peace is infinitely more difficult than waging war.

And finally, in *Foreign Bodies*, the satire is ramped up even higher as a couple seeking a bargain-priced getaway in an exotic foreign locale discover the high cost of adventurism. Its depiction of war-ravaged, dystopian chaos left in the wake of foreign military intervention in an unnamed Middle Eastern country appears markedly prescient now, more than 13 years since I wrote it, when one considers the safety and security situation inside Iraq today. I wish I wasn't able to say that.

The Iraq War itself is now consigned to history, but the lessons to be learned from it must not be. While it's now generally considered by most as a regrettable, tragic mistake, it wasn't always that way. Back in those early days of 2003, when the drumbeat of war reached *Crucible*-like levels of hysteria, spurred on by a complicit media hungry for ratings, voices of dissent were few and far between – at least in the United States – and George Orwell's *1984* doublethink phrases "War is Peace, Freedom is Slavery, Ignorance is Strength" never seemed more prophetic or more frightening.

So let us remember the past as it was, not as many might now wish to rebrand it, because, to quote Orwell once more, "Who controls the past controls the future," and if we remember the past truthfully we'll be better equipped not to repeat it.

As I write this, we once again find ourselves living through dark, troubling and uncertain times. What lies ahead of us is unknown, but if what came before has taught us anything, it is this: question everything.

May, 2017

DEDICATION

"Good enough to toss; food for powder, food for powder; they'll fill a pit as well as better"

Henry IV, Part 1

CHARACTERS

DAD: Practical-minded, carries an air of disillusionment,
           emotionally self-conscious. 40s/50s.

ROBBIE: A confident, somewhat swaggering exterior belies a
           more sweet-natured, vulnerable interior. Early 20s.

SETTING & TIME

SETTING: A graveyard.

TIME: The recent past.

Dedication had its world premiere at the Times Square Arts Center in New York in July of 2008. The play was directed by David Wells with the following cast:

Dad .... Arthur French
Robbie ....Booker T. Washington

At Rise: A small gravestone is situated downstage C., the area around it lit by a small spotlight. Kneeling in front of it, facing downstage, is DAD, his eyes fixed on the inscription that faces him. After a few moments he begins to speak.

DAD: Hello son. (*Beat.*) Not sure what I'm supposed to…well, to say in this kind of a…situation. Never was very religious, as you know. So I'm not really sure how this works. So if I miss something out…you know…sorry about that. Guess I'll just start off with the basics. So…well…hello son. (*Beat.*) I, um…I meant to come by before. Long before. But…well, you know how it is…what with your mom falling apart like she has – completely understandable, though, and I'm not complaining, but…well, it does make it harder – and work's been piling on the overtime like no one's business, and sometimes I hardly seem to get a minute to think. So what with one thing and another, it's been really hard to find the time to come by. (*Beat.*) And I suppose…I suppose if I was being honest, I've been…well, I've been putting it off a bit, too. Been thinking about you quite a bit, see, son. Quite a bit. But not here. I don't like to think of you here. I think about you how it used to be…such a short time ago. Seems like forever now. But coming here…it makes it real. Makes me face it. And the truth is, I haven't been doing all that well with this myself. Have to try, see, 'cause of your mom. But that's why you haven't seen me. Been avoiding it, I guess. But…well, here I am…and there it is…the plain truth – carved in stone.

(*A light slowly illuminates the figure of a young man, staring straight ahead, standing some distance behind DAD. After a moment he speaks.*)

ROBBIE: No flowers?

(*DAD looks up and straight ahead. For the duration of their conversation, DAD remains kneeling, ROBBIE standing some distance behind him, both looking out at the fourth wall, neither one ever looking at the other. Pause.*)

4

DAD: Sorry son?

ROBBIE: I said, no flowers? You didn't bring me any flowers.

DAD: No, I…I guess I didn't.

ROBBIE: Jeez! You finally manage to drag your sorry ass down here to see me, and when you do you can't even be bothered to bring any flowers.

DAD: Sorry about that, Robbie. Never gave it a thought. Didn't know you were that big on them, to tell you the truth.

ROBBIE: I'm not, but it's not the point. It's traditional. It's what you do when you come to these places – you bring flowers and try to brighten the place up a bit. It's like a gesture. Take a look around – they've all got 'em. Some nicer than others, but they've all got 'em. Even that slimy bastard Sammy Pearson's got flowers, and no one ever had a good to say about that lowlife ass wipe.

DAD: Easy, son. You shouldn't really speak ill of the dead, you know that.

ROBBIE: Uh, Dad…when you're one of them…*it's okay.*

DAD: Ah…yeah, I guess you gotta point there. (*Beat.*) Anyway, I'll try and bring some next time, but don't hold me to it. It's just not me, see, to go paradin' around town holdin' a big bunch of flowers like some kinda Dapper Dan. Never bought flowers before in my life. Not even for your Mom.

ROBBIE: (*Incredulous.*) Not even for Mom?

DAD: Nope, never. She understood, though.

ROBBIE: You think so, huh? Jeez, poor Mom. Man, and I thought Marines were macho.

DAD: Like I say, it's not me, but I'll try. (*Beat.*) So uh…so anyway…what's it like?

ROBBIE: What's what like?

DAD: You know…over there. Pretty decent, is it? They treatin' you okay?

ROBBIE: Ah…uh…mmm…I was kinda hopin' you wouldn't bring that up. It's not something I'm authorized to talk about, see? I'm not supposed to discuss it.

DAD: Oh right, I see…military, is it? Government stuff?

ROBBIE: Don't be a spazz, Dad. The government don't have dibs on you on the other side – though I'm sure they wish they did. No, this is more about only being privy to what goes on once you're actually here. Sort of a 'members only' thing.

DAD: Ah, yeah, I see, I see. Kinda like the mafia?

ROBBIE: Well…yeah, kind of, I guess. Only without the protection rackets and revenge killings.

DAD: Got it, got it – right. Won't ask again. Mom's the word.

ROBBIE: Talkin' of which, how's Mom doing these days?

(*Beat.*)

DAD: Well, I won't lie to you, son. She'll never be the same. She's broken. Guess we all are really. Nothing can ever be the same. When you were born we were like two little kids...we couldn't believe what had happened to us. And now...now we can't again. She buried her child. Don't get much worse.

ROBBIE: I'm all right, Dad...really I am. Know that. Tell Mom.

DAD: Maybe you are...wherever you are. I hope so. But us...we're still living with it. Trying to make sense of it. And that...the trying to make sense of it...that's the hard part.

ROBBIE: It's not that hard really. I fought and I died. And I did it for the country I loved.

DAD: I know you did, son. And we're all very proud of you. (*Beat.*) For your dedication, at any rate.

ROBBIE: "At any rate"? What the hell is that supposed to mean?

DAD: Nothin'. Nothin' really – nothin' at all. Just that in that sense – the patriotic sense –we're very, very proud of you.

ROBBIE: No, no, no...come on, you're not bein' upfront with me. Either you're proud of me or you aren't – there's no "in that sense" to it. It's black or it's white. So what are you tryin' to say?

DAD: Nothin' – really, son.

ROBBIE: C'mon, Dad, level with me.

DAD: It's not important now. It doesn't matter. You're gone...you're gone and nothing I do or say is gonna change that. Best just let it be what it is.

ROBBIE: 'Course it matters. It was my fuckin' life for chrissakes. It matters a whole lot to me, even if it's no big deal to anyone else. And I died protecting my country and protecting our freedom and our way of life – and it sure as hell don't get much more important than that!

DAD: No…no, you're right.

ROBBIE: 'Course I'm right. I don't know why you're talkin' like that. What the hell's gotten into you?

DAD: I don't know. (*Beat.*) Let's just drop it. Let's just agree and leave it at that.

ROBBIE: No, let's not agree. Let's not drop it. I'm telling you – reminding you – that I died in the course of battle for the most noble cause there is: to protect my family and my friends and everything I know and love. Why I need to remind you of this I've no idea, but I'd really appreciate it if you'd stop acting all shifty-eyed and shuffling your feet like that.

DAD: That's kinda hard when you're kneeling down.

ROBBIE: Don't get cute, you know what I mean. You're being all weird and evasive, as if…as if you don't believe in it.

DAD: Believe in what?

ROBBIE: (*Bluntly.*) What I died for.

DAD: Please, son.

ROBBIE: You don't, do you?

DAD: I told you – what does any of it matter now?

ROBBIE: It matters to me – I'm fuckin' dead!

DAD: Robbie–

ROBBIE: Do you?

DAD: Robbie, we've all had enough of it – we just want some peace.

ROBBIE: And I want a straight answer.

DAD: Why can't you just leave it alone?

ROBBIE: Why can't you answer a god damned, straightforward question when you're asked it!

DAD: Robbie, we don't–

ROBBIE: Answer me!

DAD: (*Abruptly.*) All right! All right! You want to know? Then I'll tell you. I'll damn well tell you. I'm more proud of you than anything else I've ever done, or seen, or achieved in my entire life, and I always will be – even with you gone. Nothin'll ever change that. But yours was a cheap life, son. A cheap life – thrown away by some high-paid suits in Washington playing games on an atlas. What their cause was, I couldn't tell you, but it sure as hell wasn't all that high-minded, defending a nation crap they drummed into your head before they shipped you out there.

(*Pause.*)

ROBBIE: That's bullshit!

9

DAD: It's not bullshit, son.

ROBBIE: It's total bullshit. You know damned well that's not the truth. What I'd like to know is who the hell has been fillin' your head with all that crap? You've really been taken for a ride, you know that don't you?

(*Pause.*)

ROBBIE: Don't you?

DAD: (*After a sigh.*) Well…lookin' back on it all…I guess you could say I do.

ROBBIE: Hell, Dad, I'm your son – you really think I'd be dead for no good reason?

DAD: No…no, I don't.

ROBBIE: Boy, were you taken.

DAD: Yep…taken for a fool.

ROBBIE: And now you know the truth of it?

DAD: I do now, yeah…now I know.

ROBBIE: That's it. That's more like it. That's the Dad I know. You're too smart to have a bunch of idiots pull the wool over your eyes for too long.

DAD: You'd think so, wouldn't you?

ROBBIE: I knew you'd come around.

DAD: (*Somberly.*) Oh yeah...I sure got slapped back to reality.

ROBBIE: So who was it?

DAD: Who what? What do you mean?

ROBBIE: Who was it that filled your head with all that crap?

DAD: Oh...them. Well, there was a whole bunch of 'em. All as bad as each other at the end of the day.

ROBBIE: Why the hell did ya even listen to 'em? You shoulda just told 'em to shut the fuck up right from the get go.

DAD: Yeah...I guess I should've. (*Beat.*) But they made a lot of noise, see? And they just kept sayin' the same things over and over and over again, until finally...well, I guess I just kinda believed 'em.

ROBBIE: Bastards.

DAD: Yeah. They were bastards all right.

ROBBIE: You gotta watch who you talk to out there, Dad. There's people talkin' all kinds a crazy shit, just tryin' to take advantage.

DAD: True enough.

ROBBIE: Crazy shit.

DAD: Crazy...like that yellow cake uranium in Niger.

ROBBIE: Yellow cake? What the hell are you talkin' about?

DAD: Uranium. In Niger.

ROBBIE: What the hell is Niger?

DAD: Not what – where. It's a country – in Africa.

ROBBIE: See, that's exactly what I'm talkin' about. They get your head filled with all kinds of fucked up bullshit to get ya all confused and freaked out, and before you know what's what you find yourself agreeing with 'em.

DAD: Yep, that's about how it was, my boy. That's pretty much the sum of it. (*Beat.*) First off they were jabberin' on about "weapons of mass destruction" – like they'd never existed before…like killin' a whole bunch of people with a weapon was somethin' new. But the phrase was new and it sounded good. Spooked us out at the time anyhow. So off you were packed to play their games, while we stayed behind, worryin' and stickin' magnets on our cars and pretendin' it was World War Two all over again. (*Beat.*) Only problem was…there weren't any.

ROBBIE: Dad, you know that's not what I was talkin' about when I–

DAD: Then they harped on about what a great thing it was we were doin' by toppling this bastard dictator who'd killed and tortured his own people – guess they must've picked his name out of a hat. And so on you fought…or sat…or patrolled…all the time gettin' picked off…one by one.

ROBBIE: They needed us there, Dad – they needed us there. That country was fucked up. I mean seriously fucked up!

DAD: And now?

ROBBIE: It's…it's hard. Change is hard.

DAD: Not my fight, Robbie. Not my family's.

ROBBIE: Dad, be real, they–

DAD: They said we'd be welcomed as heroes and liberators, just like back in France in '44. But they were wrong again. They played up a few scenes for the cameras and tried to convince us, but the truth of it was soon made clear enough. They just saw us for what we were – invaders. And all our big bombs and fancy technology didn't mean a damn, 'cause they went ahead and did what every other land in history's done when they've been invaded by foreigners…they turned on us.

ROBBIE: The terrorists turned on us, Dad – the extremists. The place is riddled with 'em. You don't know 'cause you weren't there, but that place is a fuckin' magnet for suicidal, whacked-out nut jobs. It's a total fuckin' madhouse.

   (*Beat.*)

DAD: But it wasn't.

ROBBIE: But it is. The whole place is one great big, fucked up, booby-trapped slice o' hell. You can't trust anything or anybody. It could all blow up in your face – someone drivin' their kids to school, a pregnant woman, a dead dog – you can't trust anything. You see people, you see all these images of ordinary people just tryin' to live their lives in the middle of all that shit…and then sometimes…sometimes it all goes crazy, and there's a flash and a boom, and you turn around and your best buddy's got his leg or his face torn off, and you scramble around, tryin' to remember what you were taught, pointing your gun at anything that moves, hopin' and prayin' that no one's got you in their sights, that there's not another blast, that none of it's real. (*Beat.*) But it is. It's a fuckin' hell n earth.

(Beat.)

DAD: But it wasn't.

ROBBIE: But it is now! It is now! And if you're in the middle of all that shit, all that death, that fear, you just gotta believe you're there for a damned good fuckin' reason. You got to – you just got to!

(Pause.)

DAD: I know…I know.

ROBBIE: Do you?

DAD: 'Course I do…did. My kid was out there…I had to. Had to hang on to something…had to believe my own flesh and blood was in danger for a god damned good reason. *(Beat.)* And then…then the story changed again and all we heard about was how they were turnin' on each other – that the whole place would go up in flames if we weren't there to keep a lid on it. A mess we'd made, but there you go – you reap what you sow. And all the news was of Arab against Arab and tribe against tribe, religion against religion, or whatever the hell their history of problems was that were now supposed to be our problems…my problems…your problems. *(Beat.)* And that's when we lost you.

(Pause.)

ROBBIE: Dad…Dad, don't say it like that. Don't put it all like that. *(Beat.)* Please don't…for me.

DAD: Like what, son?

ROBBIE: Like that…like it was…like it was all for nothin'. Like I died for nothin'.

DAD: You didn't die for nothin', son.

ROBBIE: Yes, I did…that's what you're sayin'. You're sayin' I just died. I died for some big fuck up. And I can't believe that. I can't. I have to know that I missed out on my life for a damned good fuckin' reason… (*Beat.*) And…and if you can't think of a good reason, then for god's sake go with the reasons I gave ya to begin with, 'cause…'cause I gotta believe that my life meant something, for chrissakes.

DAD: Robbie, you died believing in what was right.

ROBBIE: But it was wrong. Everything you're sayin' we went out there to do was wrong.

DAD: You didn't do wrong, Robbie. You were steered wrong, that's all. There's a big difference.

ROBBIE: (*Dismissively.*) You think so, huh?

DAD: I know so.

ROBBIE: Don't seem so big to me.

DAD: But it is. It's everything. Someone above you tells you to do something and you do it – you do your duty – 'cause you believe that they're the ones supposed to know. But that ain't always the case. (*Beat.*) I know you, Robbie. I raised you. My son was a loving, kind, honest, decent boy who believed in what was right. And if someone else took advantage of that…then shame on them.

(*Pause.*)

15

ROBBIE: Okay, if...and this is only an 'if'...and a big one...but if it's all just like you say it is, then everyone knows about it, right? And they're steamin' fuckin' angry like I am right now, right?

DAD: Well, uh...yeah, some...some are.

ROBBIE: (*Incredulous.*) Some?

DAD: People are tired of it, son.

ROBBIE: Tired?...Tired?...I'm fuckin' dead!

DAD: They're tired of bein' reminded of somethin' they'd just as soon as forget. There's a whole lot of people that got caught up in all the hoo-ha at the start that would just as soon as not be reminded that it all ended up as a big mistake. They're embarrassed – they just don't wanna think about it anymore...just wanna get on with their lives.

ROBBIE: Nice. (*Beat.*) Nice if ya got one.

DAD: I guess. (*Beat.*) I guess me and your Mom do...but it ain't much of one now. For the rest...I guess they just wanna move on. Get back to normal. Easier for them though. Our normal's gone...and it ain't comin' back.

(*Pause.*)

ROBBIE: I miss you a whole lot, Dad.

DAD: Miss you too, son.

ROBBIE: It's funny...I remember you always tellin' me how life is short and how I should always make the most of it. Heh!...you didn't know the half of it.

DAD: Well it's long on this side now, son – with things the way they are.

(*Beat.*)

ROBBIE: Tell Mom to come, okay?

DAD: I'll try. But it's all hard for her right now, you know that, yeah? All of it.

ROBBIE: I know. But tell her.

DAD: Sure I will – but I can't promise she'll come.

ROBBIE: (*His voice beginning to crack.*) Okay…but tell her. Tell her I'm here. Tell her I'm okay. Tell her I love her and…and that I'm still the same.

DAD: It's all right, son. We'll both be there with you before long, you know we will. We'll all be together again.

ROBBIE: Yep.

DAD: Maybe it'll all make a whole lot more sense over there. Sure as hell can't make any less. (*Beat.*) Anyhow…I guess I should be heading off. I'll be back to see ya again soon.

ROBBIE: (*Chidingly.*) And for chrissakes make sure you pick up some god damned flowers.

DAD: Now that I can promise ya. I won't like it but I'll do it…even if I do look like an idiot.

ROBBIE: Thanks, macho man.

DAD: So what kind do you want?

ROBBIE: Not for me, lunkhead – for Mom!

DAD: Oh…oh, yeah – good idea. I'll tell her they're from you.

ROBBIE: Bad idea. You'll tell her they're from you. That'll mean a whole lot more right now.

(*Pause.*)

DAD: Love ya, son.

ROBBIE: Yep. Right back at ya. (*Beat.*) Over and out.

(*The light on ROBBIE fades to BLACK. DAD continues to stare out ahead. After a moment or two he struggles to his feet and scans his surroundings, ensuring that no one is observing him, before raising his hand to his lips and blowing a kiss skyward.*)

DAD: Bet Marines don't do that.

(*After a brief smile, DAD turns and ambles off stage, exiting Stage R.*)

END OF PLAY

DEGRADED

CHARACTERS

AMARAH: A battered wife. Age open.

MAN: A representative from the Department of Social
   Services. Age open.

SETTING & TIME

SETTING: Amarah's living room.

TIME: The recent past.

Degraded received a developmental reading by Emerging Artists Theatre
Company at the Intar Theatre in New York in 2003.

At Rise: AMARAH sits alone on a sofa, head in hands. There is a knock at the door. She looks up with a start, her expression a look of knowing dread. The door is knocked again. Still she does not move. The door is knocked once more.

MAN: (*Off.*) Amarah? (*Pause.*) Amarah, I know you're there. (*Pause.*) Amarah, open the door.

(*AMARAH does not move. The door is knocked again.*)

MAN: (*Off.*) Amarah, open the door – please. You knew I was coming. I told you I was coming. Don't make it difficult – you know I'm here to help.

(*AMARAH'S expression is ever more tense, but still she remains seated.*)

MAN: (*Off.*) Amarah, open the door now. I'm not budging until you do. I've come a very long way to be here today and I've no intention of turning around and walking away. The Department has received information – grave information. I'm very concerned, Amarah. I don't know what's been going on in there, but I intend to find out. (*Beat.*) It's your well being I care about – I want to stop this. Now please open the door...or I promise you I'll find a way in.

AMARAH: (*Wearily.*) Won't you just go away – please? Haven't you done enough?

MAN: (*Off.*) The Department of Social Services doesn't cause problems, Amarah, we solve them, and the sooner you open this door the sooner we can resolve this crisis.

AMARAH: I'm not opening anything. I'm tired, don't you understand? I'm tired of all of you.

MAN: (*Off.*) You're weak, Amarah. You're weak and you can't think clearly. That's why I'm here – to put things in perspective; to make your life better.

AMARAH: My life would be better if you'd just leave me alone – all of you.

MAN: (*Off, forcefully.*) Amarah, open this door now and let me in. I won't ask you again.

> (*Pause. The door is knocked again. After a moment or two AMARAH drags herself up from the sofa and slowly moves toward the door. Suddenly loud thumping sounds of the door being kicked in are heard. AMARAH steps back in fear. Finally the door is kicked open and the MAN enters.*)

AMARAH: I…what are you doing! I was…this is my home!

MAN: I told you I was coming. I tried to reason with you. You wouldn't listen.

AMARAH: For God's sake, I was…this is my home – I live here! This is mine! You can't just…kick down my door!

MAN: I can – and I did.

AMARAH: On…with what right? With whose authority? I thought you wanted to help? This is…it's wrong…it's illegal.

MAN: The Department of Social Services isn't bound by any legal authority, Amarah. In cases like yours, with a proven history of spousal abuse and clear evidence of life endangerment, we operate under the auspices of the only true authority – moral authority.

AMARAH: But I don't want you here. I told you, you just make things worse.

MAN: And I told you you're not capable of thinking for yourself. How could you? You've spent so long suffering the abuse of that man, being thumped and browbeaten and belittled, that you've lost the capacity to think independently. That's why I've come – that's why they sent me – to help you regain that independence.

AMARAH: I don't want it. I don't want anything you're offering.

MAN: Of course you do – everybody does. And I'm here to give it to you.

AMARAH: By breaking into my house?

MAN: By breaking down your resistance. By breaking your dependency on a man who rules your life with an iron fist; who threatens and beats you into subservience.

AMARAH: But I...I can't...I'm too tired, I'm too weak, don't you see? I haven't the strength to fight. It's been too long.

MAN: That's why I'm here – to give you that strength. I'm on your side – surely you realize that?

AMARAH: You said that before...the last time.

MAN: And I meant it then every bit as much as I mean it now.

AMARAH: So why did you go? Why did you leave me here to face him alone?

MAN: Life's not that simple, Amarah. The Department of Social Services, however well funded, cannot be everywhere all the time –

much as we'd like to. We have outreach programs in countless communities, requiring enormous amounts of manpower and resources. Obviously there comes a point where we must expect you to begin helping yourself. If we didn't you'd simply be exchanging one dependency for another…and where would that get you?

(*Pause.*)

AMARAH: Do you know what he did to me?

MAN: We know everything.

AMARAH: After you'd gone? Do you? Do you know what he did after you came and made a big song and dance about standing up to him, about standing up for myself, about getting a divorce and starting a new life without him? Do you know what happened…after you left?

MAN: The Department can't afford to get bogged down in details, Amarah. They're a diversion. A moral crusade can only triumph by keeping its gaze fixed firmly ahead.

(*Pause. AMARAH sits on the sofa.*)

AMARAH: When you'd gone – taking your "charitable assistance" with you – I sat and I waited. I waited for him to come home, my heart pounding inside of me because I knew that he'd know that you'd been here. He seems to know everything…like you. (*Beat.*) He came in and locked the door – the same door you just destroyed – and tied my hands behind my back with the cord from the telephone and kicked my legs from beneath me. He pulled down his pants and shat on the carpet. He told me I had to eat it – all of it. (*Beat.*) I tried to breath, as much as I could, through my mouth instead of my nose as I ate so as to lessen the nausea. Still I gagged. Each time I gagged he'd kick my head…or my ribs or my legs. Finally I could stand no more and I vomited. With his boot he pushed my face into my vomit before kicking me some more. Then he left…with the feeling, I imagine, that he'd made his point.

(*Pause.*)

MAN: Words fail me, Amarah. They honestly do. How could a man do something so…unspeakable…to his own wife? How could any human being do that to another? (*Beat.*) But that's exactly why you need me now – now – don't you understand? To stop this from happening again. To stop him from ever doing that to anyone ever again. This cannot go on – it has to be stopped.

AMARAH: By who…you? Standing there in your designer suit with your Rolex watch, painting yourself out as some kindly uncle whose come to end my suffering. What do you know about suffering? What do you know of pain? What do you know of me?

MAN: I know all about you, Amarah. It's all on file…at the Department. And what we can't find out ourselves we get from your neighbors.

AMARAH: I don't believe you. They wouldn't talk to you – they're too scared of him…all of them.

MAN: Oh, they talk – quite a number of them – and they have. You'd be surprised how quickly that fear evaporates when they're reminded that their Social Services benefits could soon be subject to re-evaluation. Almost never fails. (*Beat.*) And for your information, Amarah, yes, I do know suffering. I don't enjoy talking about it, but… (*Beat.*) Almost two years ago now my brother was shot and killed while leaving a restaurant. No motive, no reason – just murdered in cold blood. Senseless killing. Some young…animal.

Some ignorant, callous, uneducated animal. From one of the poor neighborhoods, of course, and obviously full of hatred and jealousy of my brother's status in life. An immigrant at that. And so my brother's success – his hard-earned lifestyle – was brought down with a bullet to the head.

(*Beat.*)

AMARAH: (*Quietly.*) I said you.

MAN: What?

AMARAH: I said you. What do you know of suffering? Not your brother.

MAN: That isn't the issue, Amarah. The fact remains I know suffering when I see it. I know what it looks like, I know what it sounds like, and I have devoted my professional life to bringing an end to it. (*Beat. He sits on the sofa.*) I'll let you in on a little secret, shall I? But you mustn't tell anyone. This is just between us. Strictly off the record. Our little secret. (*Beat.*) You see, before the death of my brother I'd…I'd started to lose favor at the Department. They'd begun to doubt my abilities and my commitment to the job. They'd even begun to question whether they'd made a mistake in appointing me in the first place. I hate to admit it now, Amarah, but the truth is I'd started to become a little panicked. I felt embarrassed and…yes, even paranoid. You see, one of the principal reasons for my being hired in the first place was due to the long and very close relationship my family had established over the years with many prominent figures within the Department. And I couldn't let them down – I couldn't. The family name was at stake. But still I…I floundered. (*Beat.*) Then my brother was shot. Everything changed. It was profound – quite profound. But while everyone else was grieving and remembering, I…I was quietly smiling. Does that sound bad? But it's true. I smiled. I smiled because I knew – through this unimaginable tragedy – that I'd found the way forward. And I seized upon it. I ran with it, Amarah. I ran and I ran, and I'm still running…but not away – *to*.

(*Beat.*)

AMARAH: To here.

MAN: To help.

AMARAH: To interfere.

MAN: To solve.

(*Beat.*)

AMARAH: (*Determinedly.*) Go.

MAN: (*With a steely look.*) No.

(*Beat.*)

AMARAH: (*Very deliberately.*) Try to believe me – I don't care what you say your motives are, you're not wanted here. (*Beat.*) You say my life's in danger – and it is – only more so now because of you. You say I don't understand – I don't. I don't understand you. How can you possibly say I don't understand my circumstances when I'm living them each and every day? I live in fear. I live in an atmosphere filled with suspicion and recrimination. But I've adapted – I've had to. And some day I'll…perhaps I'll find the strength to escape it. Perhaps one day he'll die of a heart attack, or I'll…or my friends will…something…somehow. But that's for me to decide. But you can't speak for me – you don't know my life. You have your facts and

31

figures and your hearsay. You mouth your words so benevolently with that compassionate smile. You have a title and you have power but you understand nothing.

MAN: Amarah, I understand you. I understand the pain and humiliation you live with every moment of your life. And it kills me inside, Amarah – it kills me. You deserve so much better. (*As he puts his arm around her.*) So much better.

AMARAH: (*With a start.*) What are you doing?

MAN: Comforting you.

AMARAH: (*Pulling away.*) Don't.

MAN: (*Pulling her closer.*) Amarah, I'm here – for you.

AMARAH: (*Resisting.*) I don't want you here, I told you – go!

MAN: (*Pulling her to him more forcefully.*) Don't fight it, Amarah – I just want to make it better.

AMARAH: (*Desperately trying to pull away.*) Get off of me!

MAN: Amarah – don't make it more difficult. I'm much stronger than you are – you'll just make it worse for yourself. I'll win in the end – you know I will.

AMARAH: (*Struggling.*) Win what? Stop! Get away from me!

MAN: (*Locking her firmly in his embrace.*) Amarah, relax – just let me do what must be done.

AMARAH: Please! I can't…why are you doing this?

MAN: To free you. To make your life better. I'm doing this for you.

(*AMARAH suddenly manages to free one of her arms and forcibly pushes the MAN'S face away from her. The MAN slaps her violently across the face, causing her to cry out in pain.*)

MAN: Stop it! I'm helping you!

AMARAH: (*Feebly.*) Please. Please, I beg you – just leave me alone. I don't want this.

MAN: (*As he pushes her to the floor.*) Of course you do. Everybody does. My way is the right way, the only way – the best way. You only think you don't because you've never felt it.

(*The MAN rips open AMARAH'S clothing, and unzips his pants.*)

AMARAH: (*With a loud scream.*) No!

(*The MAN slaps AMARAH hard across the face and proceeds to rape her.*)

MAN: They all want it, but…ahh…they don't always know it because…ohh…they've never known any different. They…have no experience of it, you see? No real experience of…ahh…what we have, what we're like, what we offer. But now you know…oh, Amarah…doesn't it feel good? Doesn't it make you feel alive? I mean really alive? Can you feel it? Can you…ahh…can you feel it – deep down inside? That's it, Amarah. That's freedom – that's what it feels like, that's…oh, God, doesn't it feel good? Feel that! That's life! That's life beyond him! That's your new life! That's the end of an era! That's the beginning of the end! That's the end of history! That's starting from now! That's me in you! That's…that's… (*With a sigh of satisfaction he reaches orgasm.*) Liberty.

(Pause. The MAN pulls himself up from the floor as AMARAH begins to weep.)

MAN: Yes, Amarah, cry. Let it out. Let out all the pain. Let out all the suffering. Then cry some more…with a smile on your face. Tears of happiness. Happiness at being born again. For the life we'll show you. For all you've left behind. For what's to come. Cry your tears and wipe them away. Wipe it all away. Cleanse yourself – of the past, of him. Your past is dirty. Your past is shameful. Your past is irrelevant now. We'll show you a new life. Your life begins now – nothing came before. You're like a baby in the cradle. We'll care for you. We'll supply you with all that you need. We'll shape you. We'll make you. *(Beat.)* Feel's good, doesn't it? Come on, give me a smile.

AMARAH: *(Weakly.)* Do whatever you want.

MAN: *(Distractedly.)* Yes… *(Suddenly.)* Yes! I almost forgot.

(The MAN hurriedly exits L. AMARAH attempts to drag herself up from the floor, grasping at the sofa cushions, before giving up and burying her head in her arms. Soon the MAN reappears with a can of gasoline and begins dousing its contents around the room.)

AMARAH: *(Looking up.)* What are you doing?

MAN: Ending this.

AMARAH: Ending what?

MAN: This. This haven of hatred and evil deeds. I'm erasing it.

AMARAH: *(Standing.)* But…but you're insane? This is my home!

MAN: It's a building, Amarah – a structure. Nothing more. The

Department will find you a new one – modern – one you'll be happy in.

AMARAH: But I live here! Everything I have is here!

MAN: (*Derisively.*) What do you have?

AMARAH: Everything! My furniture – my clothes!

MAN: Replaceable. All of it. What you have is junk anyway. It's all old fashioned. Hate to sound condescending, Amarah, but...well, I can't lie to you.

AMARAH: But it's mine.

MAN: You've got to stop living in the past, Amarah. That's the problem with cases like yours – you're stuck some other time. You keep clinging to those old memories as if they still meant something. The smile of reassurance on your wedding day. The words of commitment. The promise of a brighter future. You forget all the beatings, the screams, the insults, the forced sex and the fake apologies. That was the old you – this is the new you.

AMARAH: (*Pleading.*) But my things...my photographs, my letters...my passport. At least let me get my passport. It's the only thing that's really mine.

MAN: (*Putting down the gasoline can.*) What do you need with a passport? You're not going anywhere. Well, you are, but...you won't need a passport.

AMARAH: (*Reaching out to him.*) Please...just one or two things.

MAN: Best to start anew.

AMARAH: But I need to remember.

MAN: Best to forget.

AMARAH: But how shall I go on?

MAN: With faith, Amarah – faith in us. We'll take care of you. You'll have a new home, an allowance – all your basic needs supplied by the Department. (*As he reaches into his pocket.*) The Department's standards of just means of support are the finest in the world. We will, of course, expect you to make every effort yourself to ensure your future prosperity…in other words, we'll expect a little something in return. And I have every confidence in you, Amarah – I do. But if you stumble…if you weaken or go astray…I'll always be there for you. (*Beat. As he puts his arms around her.*) I promise. Just as I have been today. You have my word.

AMARAH: (*Desolately.*) I just want it to end. I can't fight anymore.

MAN: (*Producing a book of matches from his left hand, his voice ever more zealous.*) And so it will. You'll forget all of this. The nightmare is over. You'll be reborn. Growth is painful, Amarah. Sacrifices must be made. There's a price to pay. The price of freedom. Your freedom. It's a state of mind. It's a state of independence. Here in my arms. Can you feel it? In these arms. These arms of absolution. Do you feel it? Do you feel the strength of my arms. The power. The might. My arms. Your life. My arms. Your body. Can you feel it? Can you feel my arms? Can you? (*Forcefully.*) Can you!

AMARAH: (*In a cry of desperation.*) Stop it!

(*The MAN places a hand over AMARAH'S mouth.*)

MAN: Shhh! No more words. Your words have no meaning. I'll do the talking. You do the smiling. Smile for me, Amarah. Smile and show me that you're happy. Smile for me. Kiss me. Show me a little gratitude. Show me that you're glad I came. Show me that you love me. You're free, Amarah! I've given you freedom! Show me your happiness! Kiss me! Show me! Love me! (*As he pulls her around to face him.*) You're mine now.

(*Locking his mouth against hers, the MAN reaches his arms around AMARAH'S back, pulls a match from the book and strikes. BLACKOUT.*)

END OF PLAY

THE JONESES

"It is not enough to win a war; it is more important to organize the peace."

— Aristotle

CHARACTERS

MR. JONES: Intransigent, pragmatic, with a zealous edge.
              Middle-aged.

MRS. JONES: Highly-strung, somewhat affected, occasionally
              revealing an inner resentment. Middle-aged.

SETTING & TIME

SETTING: A living room.

TIME: The recent past.

The Joneses was awarded semi-finalist honors in the 11th Annual
National One-Act Play Competition by First Stage in Hollywood in
2007.

At Rise: MR. JONES .is sitting in an armchair, Stage R., his head buried in a newspaper. Presently, MRS. JONES enters from Stage L. in an extremely agitated state, slamming the door behind her.

MRS. JONES: That's it! I've had enough! They've tried my patience one too many times today and now I've just about had it! There's nothing more I can do – I give up!

MR. JONES: (*Without looking up.*) Something wrong, Mrs. Jones?

MRS. JONES: It doesn't matter what I say, nothing makes a blind bit of difference. I may as well be talking to a brick wall.

MR. JONES: Is it the children again?

MRS. JONES: Of course it's the children. When is it not the children? I never get a minute's peace with those two. It's one long constant battle of wills.

MR. JONES: Well I'm sure they'll soon settle down if you just let them be for a while.

MRS. JONES: Let them be? How on earth am I supposed to do that when they're hell bent on beating the living daylights out of each other?

MR. JONES: Boys will be boys, Mrs. Jones. You can't expect them to behave like model children all of the time.

MRS. JONES: I just need a little peace and quiet. Is that really so much to ask?

MR. JONES: Parenthood brings with it all manner of responsibilities, some of them none too pleasant. We'd acknowledged and agreed that it wasn't likely to be all plain sailing long before we made the decision to adopt.

MRS. JONES: I am fully aware of what my responsibilities are, thank you all the same. But I wonder, Mr. Jones…are you?

MR. JONES: What are you implying?

MRS. JONES: Well, you're supposed to be the man of the house, aren't you? Why don't you try doing something about it, instead of just sitting there ogling the sports pages?

MR. JONES: Perhaps because I know when to leave well enough alone. Mark my words, it'll all blow over if you just let them sort it out amongst themselves.

(Just then several loud sounds of things crashing and banging are heard offstage.)

MRS. JONES: Oh how right you are. The spirit of reconciliation never sounded sweeter. My apologies for ever doubting your word.

MR. JONES: I fail to see how resorting to sarcasm is going to improve matters.

MRS. JONES: But what are we going to do, for heaven's sake? We can't just let them pulverize each other into the ground.

MR. JONES: I think you're making rather more of this than is absolutely necessary.

MRS. JONES: But listen to what they're doing to each other in there! They're not just unruly, they're unhinged. We are their parents. We have a responsibility for their safety and wellbeing, and what's happening in that room right now is simply not normal!

MR. JONES: May I remind you, Mrs. Jones, that our little darlings originate from a gene pool of which we know absolutely nothing about. Moreover, the culture from which we rescued them is vastly different to our own, and I think it behoves us to remain sensitive to some of their ethnic idiosyncrasies, however cruel they may appear to us. For all we know, this may be their way of bonding. And as much as we may desire to bestow our superior lifestyle upon them, we have to accept that they're going to have their little ways.

(*Just then, more loud crashes and bangs are heard offstage.*)

MRS. JONES: Little ways? That's putting it mildly. (*Sitting in the armchair L.*) I had no idea motherhood would be so traumatizing.

MR. JONES: Well what is it they're fighting about exactly? What's the problem here?

MRS. JONES: Oh, I don't know – it's always something different. Then again, it all amounts to the same thing. Last week it was the bunk bed. Ali, being a year older, decided that he should be the one in the top bunk. Omar, having gotten used to being there, refused to budge. Pandemonium and mayhem ensued, of course, until finally Ali got his way. Now Omar's refusing to share the same room with him and it's become a full-scale conflict to see who can force the other out. They've taken to strangling each other in the middle of the night.

MR. JONES: Then perhaps you're not thinking far enough outside of the box. Why don't you suggest to them that they divide the room into separate sections, each with its own half of the bunk? That way they can both feel important.

MRS. JONES: It wouldn't make a jot of difference. It's not about sharing, it's about control. Omar wants Ali out and vice versa. Each thinks the other should sleep in the study from hereon, and both seem willing to stop at nothing in order to make that a reality.

MR. JONES: I am not having my study turned into a bedroom! That is sacred ground! Some of my greatest thinking is done in that room.

MRS. JONES: Oh calm down. No one's asking you to give up your study, I'm just trying to illustrate the gravity of a situation that, whether through negligence or wantonness, you have thus far seemed completely oblivious to.

(*More loud smashing and banging is heard offstage.*)

MR. JONES: (*Cautiously.*) Then I think the time may have come for us to consider employing a little d-i-s-c-i-p-l-i-n-e.

MRS. JONES: You needn't bother spelling it out. They can't hear you from here, they wouldn't understand, and more to the point, they wouldn't care, either. Trust me, I've tried every means at my disposal and nothing seems to make an impact. The minute I turn my head they're back at it again.

MR. JONES: (*Reprovingly.*) Spare the rod, spoil the child, Mrs. Jones, that's how I was raised.

MRS. JONES: I haven't spared the rod! Good God, I've yelled and screamed at them until I've made myself hoarse, but it doesn't make the slightest difference.

MR. JONES: What about a curfew?

MRS. JONES: (*With an air of exasperation.*) Doesn't work, I've tried it. I've locked them in their room, I've put pillowcases over their heads,

I've bound their wrists and ankles together with jump rope, I've made them stand on their lunchboxes for hours at a time until their muscles gave out, I've even set the dog on them. I mean, what else is a mother supposed to do? Tell me!

MR. JONES: Now, now, don't get yourself all worked into a state. Just like anything else, child rearing has its obstacles, but I'm quite sure it'll all sort itself out if we keep our heads and stop focusing on the negative all the time.

MRS. JONES: You keep saying that, but I can't help having this nagging suspicion that we've bitten off far more than we can chew.

MR. JONES: That's defeatist talk and I will hear no more of it. A firm hand and a steely jaw are all that's needed to prevail, just you wait and see.

(*MRS. JONES rises and begins nervously pacing the room.*)

MRS. JONES: Oh, I suppose you're right. I don't know what to think anymore. It's just that I'd had such high hopes for all of this. I'd always imagined our neighbors looking upon us as the ultimate parents, setting an example of just what can be accomplished when two privileged, determined individuals wrap their arms around a couple of scraggly little souls from some barbaric outpost of humanity and turn them into something shiny and new. (*With a sigh.*) It sounds silly now, but I'd even dreamt of being looked upon as something of a visionary; of my name being mentioned only in the most hushed and hallowed of tones. (*Beat.*) Now I fear we'll be seen as nothing more than two meddling, bungling fools who orchestrated a disaster, all in the name of their own vanity. Oh, what have we done, Mr. Jones? What have we done?

MR. JONES: Stop talking like that! I won't hear of it. I refuse to let the antics of a couple of scruffy little Third World sand rats taint our standing and reputation in this community as generous, warm-hearted benefactors. Now, there are bound to be bumps in the road – that's only to be expected. But we cannot allow a little over-excitedness on the part of our beloved children to throw off our moral compass. After all, at the end of the day it's just a little sibling rivalry.

MRS. JONES: Perhaps that's half the problem? Perhaps if we'd picked two from the same family we wouldn't be having to endure all of this mayhem.

MR. JONES: Well, it's too late now. We can't start second guessing ourselves. What's done is done.

MRS. JONES: And I'd hardly call it "sibling rivalry." Last week I caught Ali drilling holes in Omar's leg with your Black & Decker drill. The week before, I discovered Omar…well, I'd rather not go into it before dinner. Suffice to say that every time I take them to the emergency room, I find the hospital staff giving me stranger and stranger looks. I'd almost say they were accusatory…as if I were somehow to blame.

MR. JONES: Then perhaps it's time we thought about bringing in some help; someone who can share the blame. I mean, er…the responsibility.

MRS. JONES: You mean like a nanny or an au pair?

MR. JONES: Yes. Someone cheap from abroad.

MRS. JONES: But I thought I told you – I interviewed several qualified individuals last week for just such a position and none of them were interested. They took one look at Omar and Ali having at it and bolted for the door.

MR. JONES: Damn! All of them?

MRS. JONES: Well, there was one willing to offer her services – a rather gruesome looking woman from Uzbekistan with hairy forearms – but quite frankly her terms were outlandish.

MR. JONES: Then to hell with them! We'll go it alone, just you and me. We'll show them all.

MRS. JONES: Easy for you to say, you're the one with his head buried in the sports pages half the day. I'm the one out there on the front lines having to deal with this madness.

(More banging sounds, followed by a bloodcurdling scream.)

MR. JONES: And you've been doing a spectacular job, Mrs. Jones. No one could be more proud of you than I am. But I think it's worth remembering that adopting children is a very big undertaking. It's not quite the same as having a pet – you can't simply send them back to the shelter once they start making puddles on the carpet.

MRS. JONES: (With a deep sigh.) Oh, sometimes I just wish we could. I know it's awful to admit, but it's true.

MR. JONES: It's also completely impossible, so I suggest you banish the thought from your mind at the earliest opportunity.

MRS. JONES: (With a slightly bitter tone.) I know it's impossible. (Beat.) I also recall the reason why.

MR. JONES: I see. So we're back to throwing that in my face, are we?

MRS. JONES: I'm not throwing anything in your face; I was simply reminding myself that I was not the one with a history of substance abuse.

MR. JONES: For the umpteenth time, Mrs. Jones, it was a foible of youth!

MRS. JONES: Yes, and one that got us turned down by every legitimate adoption agency in Christendom.

MR. JONES: Mr. Qasim's services were entirely professional and utterly beyond reproach. I read all of his references and I still maintain we had no reason to doubt him.

MRS. JONES: Clearly not. Look, why don't we just face the truth — we were willing to accept just about anything that conniving little crook told us, however ludicrous, because we were so damned desperate to get our hands on those children and prove something to the world. (*Beat.*) And now look at us…a laughing stock.

> (*Just then an enormous crash is heard, along with the sound of breaking glass, followed by another bloodcurdling scream.*)

MR. JONES: (*Standing abruptly.*) We are *not* a laughing stock, we are *not* defeatists, and we *will* make this work. Together, you and I are going to demonstrate to our dear friends and neighbors just exactly what it is that makes us superior to them. Oh, I know they're all peeking from behind their curtains, just waiting for us to fail. I hear all the snickering and the sniping and the muttering of "I told you so" under their breath. Don't think it passes me by. But they'll be smiling on the other side of their faces by the time we're through. Mark my words, between you, me and the good grace of the Almighty, we're going to make those bastards eat shit.

(*MRS. JONES crosses to her husband and puts her arms around him.*)

MRS. JONES: Oh, Mr. Jones, do you really think it's possible?

MR. JONES: (*With a resolute outward gaze.*) It's more than possible, it's inevitable. It's destiny.

MRS. JONES: I do so hope you're right. When you first suggested all of this to me, I must confess I did have my misgivings. But I tried to hide them because I…because I wanted to make you happy, and because…well, because a part of me felt inadequate, if you must know. I felt ashamed because I couldn't give you those children. (*Beat.*) There was a time, of course, way back when, in the days when I was still young and vital…when it seemed as though the sun would never set. But when I met you it was already too late. I was already past my prime. Just a barren trophy wife from a good family with a respected name.

MR. JONES: A damned fine name. You gave me instant cachet. I couldn't have asked for better.

MRS. JONES: (*With a loving embrace.*) And neither could I. Suddenly it seemed as if all my schoolgirl dreams had come true. There I was, about to be married to the wealthiest, most powerful man in the community. And I knew that together we'd be even stronger. This was not going to be any run-of-the-mill union of two people, this was…this was something special.

MR. JONES: Very special.

MRS. JONES: Everyone could tell.

MR. JONES: They knew it.

MRS. JONES: And when the children came along – well, when we procured them – I thought that our stature would only be enhanced, as if that were possible. I imagined people to be awestruck by our largesse; to marvel at our determination to share everything we cherish and hold dear with two impoverished little urchins from the lands of the mystics. (*Beat.*) Could it really all have been a dream just out of reach?

MR. JONES: Ah, but dreams need to be believed in if you wish to keep them alive. You keep rounding back to reality, Mrs. Jones, but no good will come of it. Believe me, it's a mistake.

(*Suddenly more deafening noise is heard, followed by several gunshots and a sickening scream.*)

MRS. JONES: But just listen to them, Mr. Jones. That is not the sound of a happy home.

MR. JONES: It's the sound of change. Pay them no mind – you just keep dreaming the dream.

MRS. JONES: (*Becoming tearful.*) Could it be that we've…we've failed as parents?

MR. JONES: No! Now just you listen to me. We have given those wild-eyed little carpetbaggers the opportunity of a lifetime. Before we intervened in their lives they were living some miserable, hand-to-mouth existence in that godforsaken, armpit of a country, under the tutelage of shamans. What we did for those boys was nothing short of a miracle. Good God, Mrs. Jones, there are literally millions of dark-skinned little wretches roaming the savannahs of Africa that would have offered up a limb to have what they have. But no, we chose Omar and Ali…and this is the thanks we get. So I say to hell with them! Let them sort it out for themselves. We've done all we can.

MRS. JONES: But we can't just abandon them. It would be pure chaos in there.

(*MR. JONES throws her a look of irony.*)

MRS. JONES: (*Wearily.*) Well…I suppose it does seem rather ungrateful.

MR. JONES: Ungrateful? It's the height of ignorance. Let them beat each other to a pulp. They can rip each other to shreds for all I care. This mess is as much their responsibility as it is ours and it's high time they took ownership. If they don't learn now they never will.

MRS. JONES: And it's true we can only guide them so far, after all.

MR. JONES: Personal responsibility, Mrs. Jones.

MRS. JONES: And I suppose these things do have a way of sorting themselves out sometimes.

MR. JONES: Of course they do. You just have to give it time. It all comes right in the end. You just have to keep believing. Keep the dream alive, Mrs. Jones. Live the dream. Live and breathe it. Let it fill your mind.

MRS. JONES: Yes, I…I am beginning to feel a little fuzzy, actually.

MR. JONES: That's it, that's the spirit – open yourself up to it.

MRS. JONES: No, I mean…I'm starting to feel a bit odd. (*Sniffing the air.*) Do you smell something?

MR. JONES: I don't smell a thing.

MRS. JONES: It…it smells like smoke. (*Sniffing the air again.*) Is something burning?

(*Very gradually the lights slowly begin turning redder and redder.*)

MR. JONES: The only thing that's burning is the beacon of hope that you and I have lit for our blessed children.

MRS. JONES: It definitely smells like smoke to me.

MR. JONES: (*Clutching her to his side and pointing out ahead.*) Look to the light, Mrs. Jones, and believe in its promise of a brighter tomorrow. There's a new sun rising on a world where everything is right again, and we shall bask in its warmth and glory.

MRS. JONES: Yes, it…it is starting to get a little warm in here. Are you sure you can't smell anything?

(*The crackling sounds of a fire can be heard, as the lights grow increasingly redder.*)

MR. JONES: It's the smell of victory, Mrs. Jones. It's the smell of all our naysaying neighbors eating their words. It's the smell of every malcontent and turncoat friend fuming at the prospect of our glorious success as proud parents. Breathe it in – breathe it deep into your lungs!

MRS. JONES: (*After a deep breath, followed by a coughing fit.*) It's…it's rather pungent, isn't it? (*Between coughs.*) I say, those…those boys are awfully quiet. I do hope they're not…not making mischief.

MR. JONES: Why worry about them? Just look! Look to the light! Have you ever seen a sight more magnificent? Just look at it – bursting with the hope of a brighter future. Give into it, Mrs. Jones. Accept it. Breathe it in, breathe it in deep. Have you ever smelled anything so intoxicating?

MRS. JONES: (*Coughing heavily.*) No, I…I…actually, I…oh…

(*MRS. JONES faints and drops to the floor. MR. JONES raises his arms to the sky, the lights flooding the stage with red, the sound of flames growing ever louder.*)

MR. JONES: Yes, Mrs. Jones, throw yourself before Him! Oh thank you, Lord! Thank you for this unshakeable will you've given us. Thank you for bestowing upon us the strength and determination to stand firm in the face of the incredulous. Your words have been my weapons. I am yours, your humble servant, your vessel, your instrument of change. My children are now your children, freed from the grasp of the wailing pagans, free to embrace their new life. And we'll help them; we'll teach them and tame them. Oh, how happy they'll be! Educated and integrated, anglicised and circumcised. They'll dance and sing and praise the day the heavens opened up and changed their world forever. Oh, what model children they'll be, such model children. An example to the world! And they will call me father, and they will take my name, and they will be my legacy when I am gone, these children of the sand. Oh thank you, dear Lord, for leading me on this path, for bringing me to this place. I feel you here. I feel the warmth of your breath, the fire of your passion, the red hot glow of your unending embrace. (*Beat.*) I am with you now, here where I belong. I've come home…home to you.(*Beat.*) You knew I'd come. And I knew you'd be waiting…waiting here for me. (*Beat.*) Waiting with your baptismal fires; your eternal flames. Waiting in that light that never goes out…never goes out.

(The lights fade to BLACK.)

END OF PLAY

FOREIGN BODIES

"In war, the strong make slaves of the weak, and in peace the rich makes slaves of the poor."

— Oscar Wilde

CHARACTERS

VICTORIA: Insouciant, somewhat naïve, with a fondness for prescription drugs. 40s/50s.

MAX: A cantankerous cynic whose blustering demeanour belies a timorous interior. 40s/60s.

SETTING & TIME

SETTING: A hotel balcony in an unspecified foreign locale.

TIME: The present.

Foreign Bodies had its world premiere at New York's Theatre Row in April of 2005, produced by Emerging Artists Theatre Company. The play was directed by Dylan McCullough with the following cast:

Victoria .... Laura Fois
Max .... Kurt Kingsley

At Rise: A hotel room exterior with French doors opening up to a decorative patio overlooking the sea. VICTORIA enters through the French doors, walks downstage to the edge of the balcony and takes a large inhalation of breath.

VICTORIA: Ahh… (*Beat.*) Oh, Darling, I can hardly believe that we're here. It seems like only yesterday we were moping about under yet another "overcast, but likely to improve," High Wycombe sky.

MAX: (*Emerging from the French doors.*) Probably because we were. Unless it's slipped your mind, we only arrived last night.

VICTORIA: Oh, Max, how can you be so literal-minded in a place like this? Just look… (*Gesturing at the sights before her.*) Look at all of that.

MAX: (*Grudgingly.*) Mmm…very nice.

VICTORIA: It's…it's like another world. It's…transcendental, or…metaphysical, or…something. Oh damn, I wish I were more poetic at times like this.

MAX: Frankly, it's a relief you're not.

VICTORIA: (*Lost in thought.*) How can it be so different? Just a short hop on a plane and it's as if one were on another planet. Everything seems so new – re-fashioned and turned upside down. I think it's the most wonderful sensation a person can have: to know it's all so much bigger and stranger than what you thought it was.

MAX: Did you pack the nail clippers?

VICTORIA: What?

MAX: The nail clippers. These sandals expose my toes and…well, in

63

a pair of Oxfords I can skip a few weeks, but in these it's all…well, it's public. Wouldn't want to give off the wrong signals.

VICTORIA: To whom?

MAX: Well…the local populace, I suppose. Don't want them to get the wrong impression.

VICTORIA: I'd be surprised if your toenails held much interest for them, but there's a pair in my vanity case.

MAX: Which is?

VICTORIA: The forest green and burnt umber chequered Louis Vuitton personal accessory you gave me on our last anniversary which is situated on the dresser next to my harmony pills.

MAX: Oh no, Victoria, not your bloody harmony pills again. Why did you have to bring those wretched things with you? I told you to leave them behind. This is meant to be a break from all that. What good is it if you're going to drag all your baggage along with you?

VICTORIA: It's not baggage, it's vital medication.

MAX: The whole *point* of a holiday is to provide one with a harmonious experience. Why bother if you're going to be drugged and popping pills every second of it.

VICTORIA: Oh stop being such an old crank and cut your nails.

MAX: (*As he exits back through the French doors.*) I've half a mind to flush them down the toilet.

VICTORIA: (*Calling after him.*) Don't you dare! (*Returning her gaze to the sights before her and sighing contentedly.*) Oh honestly, Max, it's like a dream…a mirage. It's all so hypnotic and mysterious and unfamiliar…and just a teeny bit dangerous. (*Beat.*) I wonder if the local inhabitants realise just how fortunate they are? Probably not. I expect they're too busy bartering their olives and trinkets and whatnot to think about how beautiful their life is. It's a shame really. (*Ruefully.*) I'm sure they'd soon change their tune if they spent a few cold, grey, wet Saturday afternoons in High Wycombe…on their own…while their husband worked overtime…once again.

MAX: (*Off.*) Darling, did you call room service and order the cosmopolitans as I asked you?

VICTORIA: Yes, I did.

MAX: (Off.) Then why aren't they here?

VICTORIA: (*Dreamily, to herself.*) Were I were room service I would be more than happy to give you a definitive answer to that question. As it is, I'm afraid all I can do is…gaze in wonder at this blazing azure sky and ponder upon the inexplicable nature of my existence.

MAX: (*Off.*) Call them again then, would you?

VICTORIA: In a minute.

MAX: (*Off.*) It's intolerably hot. A man has to have something to – ow!

VICTORIA: (*Looking back at the room.*) Are you all right?

MAX: (*Off.*) Yes, yes, just…cut a bit close to the quick. Ooh…ahh…

VICTORIA: (*Looking out before her again.*) Yes…I know the feeling.

MAX: (*Off.*) What?

VICTORIA: Does it need a bandage or something?

MAX: (*Off.*) No, no, no, there's no blood. It just hurts to high bloody heaven.

VICTORIA: Yes.

(*MAX re-enters the balcony, limping slightly.*)

MAX: A fine impression this is giving the natives. I'd have been better off letting them think I had claws.

VICTORIA: Are you sure it doesn't require some sort of medical attention?

MAX: It didn't even cut the flesh, Victoria. It's not an emergency, it's just bloody painful. If they'd only hurry up with those wretched drinks I'm sure I'd feel a damned sight better.

VICTORIA: I can call them again if you like but they were very rude.

MAX: Rude?

VICTORIA: Yes, very. I think he swore at me – but I couldn't swear on it.

MAX: God, that infuriates me! These people learn some archaic foreign language and then assume they have full license to get one up on you!

VICTORIA: Now don't get all in a tizz. Perhaps he didn't. Perhaps it was some sort of ethnic blessing and I misunderstood.

MAX: I don't trust any of them.

VICTORIA: It was just the tone of his voice.

MAX: If they don't want our business or our currency then they should damned well come out and say it. I'm not going to be holed up in here with you for an entire week if all the thanks I get is to be spat on.

VICTORIA: Oh, I…I thought you…

MAX: What?

VICTORIA: I don't know, I…I thought the reason we came here *was* for you to spend some time with me.

MAX: Well…it was – *is*. But that's not the point.

VICTORIA: Then what is?

MAX: The point, Victoria, is that by choosing to spend a holiday here we are actively contributing to the betterment of these people's lives. Our disposable income, in its own modest way, is helping to rebuild their shattered economy and alleviate their hand-to-mouth existence. I had hoped that a reciprocal gesture might've been in order, but apparently it's all a one-way street.

VICTORIA: (*Looking down over the balcony.*) Is it really? How terribly confusing.

MAX: I was speaking metaphorically.

VICTORIA: Yes, I can see that. (*Beat.*) Oh! Oh, look! (*Pointing toward the ground.*) Darling, look, look! Quick!

MAX: (*Dispassionately.*) What is it?

VICTORIA: It's a…oh, darling look, it's a…a small one.

MAX: A what?

VICTORIA: A small…a little one…of them. Quick!

MAX: (*Leaning over the balcony.*) That?

VICTORIA: Yes.

MAX: It's a child.

VICTORIA: Yes…but of them…a small one. Oh, how sweet. It's the first one I've seen. (*Waving her hand.*) Hello!

MAX: I'm sure it won't be the last.

VICTORIA: Oh, how adorable! Throw it something.

MAX: What?

VICTORIA: Throw it something. Throw something down.

MAX: Like what?

VICTORIA: Some coins or something.

MAX: (*Feeling in his pockets.*) I don't have any.

VICTORIA: Oh, then anything – it doesn't matter. It'll be grateful.

MAX: I've nothing on me.

VICTORIA: (*Looking about her.*) Oh, just…throw it that ashtray.

MAX: (*Picking up a large glass ashtray from the patio table.*) This thing?

VICTORIA: Yes, yes, it's shiny – it'll like it. Just throw it. Quick, before it goes!

MAX: All right.

(*MAX tosses the ashtray over the edge of the balcony. Beat.*)

VICTORIA: (*With some concern.*) Oh.

MAX: (*With a grimace.*) Ouch. That's a bit unfortunate.

VICTORIA: Darling, I meant you to throw something *to* it not *at* it.

MAX: Well don't blame me, I don't have a laser-guided wrist.

VICTORIA: Do you think it's all right?

MAX: Yes, I'm sure it is. I expect it just…needs a little time to recover, that's all.

VICTORIA: But it's not moving.

MAX: That's the way they are here – none of them move very much.

(*Just then a crackling sound of gunfire is heard.*)

VICTORIA: (*Jumping, somewhat panicked.*) What was that?

MAX: (*Shaken but resolute.*) Not sure…crickets probably.

VICTORIA: Crickets? That loud?

MAX: In this part of the world, yes. It's the climate and... what have you. Hybrids and all that. Nothing to be alarmed about.

VICTORIA: Nevertheless, that sounded rather close to home. Did you bring the repellent?

MAX: I think I did.

VICTORIA: Then would you fetch it for me, darling – I'm starting to feel a little less enchanted than I was just now.

MAX: Well, I'll look but I can't swear that I–

VICTORIA: No, no, on second thoughts just bring me my harmony pills, would you? And a bottle of mineral water from the mini-bar.

MAX: I'm not bringing you those damned things! I paid good money for this holiday and I'm bloody determined to see you enjoy every minute of it – however painful.

VICTORIA: Max, I must have something – I can feel my nerves starting to fray.

MAX: (*Crossing back to the room.*) All this fuss over a few bloody insects. I'll find that damned repellent if it kills me.

VICTORIA: (*Calling after him.*) Darling, if they're hybrids it's probably not strong enough anyway. It's just a cheapie I picked up at Boots. Just bring me my pills – that way I won't have to worry about it.

MAX: (*Off.*) I want you to worry! That's real life!

VICTORIA: (*Looking back out across the balcony.*) I think I do enough of that already – with or without the pills. (*Beat.*) And it's not simply a matter of it being someone else. Someone else I could cope with, I suppose…eventually…in a sad way. It's just the age. The youth. I thought after all this time…those times…some good, some bad…that somehow it all mattered – at least on aggregate. But it didn't. I can be pushed aside over something as facile as age. (*Beat.*) Then again, I suppose all those years did matter – just in the wrong way. (*Beat.*) Now, that's real life.

MAX: (*Off.*) Did you pack it or did I?

VICTORIA: (*Looking back to the room.*) What?

MAX: (*Off.*) The insect repellent.

VICTORIA: You must've.

MAX: (*Off.*) I can't find it.

VICTORIA: Then I must've.

MAX: (*Off.*) Then where is it?

VICTORIA: I don't know. Probably still at home. (*Beat. Looking back across the balcony.*) Home. There's a thought. And not a pleasant one, conjuring up as it does all sorts of images – and none that I wish to dwell on. Not now, at least.

MAX: (*Off.*) Damn this infernal hole. Why is it so hot in here?

VICTORIA: It's not out here, darling – it's rather lovely.

MAX: (*Off.*) Something as simple as electricity and they can't keep it

71

running for more than a bloody hour at a time. Why install air-conditioning if you can never use it?

VICTORIA: A little balmy, but I'd be disappointed if it wasn't.

MAX: (*Off.*) Oh, to hell with it!

VICTORIA: (*Peering at something in the distance.*) Oh, look…it's a…sort of a…oh, what's it called?

MAX: (*Emerging from the room.*) What are you jabbering on about?

VICTORIA: There, look. (*Pointing before her.*) It's a…those little islands, they're a…oh, rats! What's that word? I can never remember it.

MAX: I don't see them.

VICTORIA: (*Pointing again.*) There. Just there below that lonely little cloud.

MAX: (*Pointing.*) What, that?

VICTORIA: Archipelago!

MAX: That right there?

VICTORIA: Why can I never remember that word? It's so unique you'd think it would be hard not to. (*Excitedly.*) Anyway, not only do we have an ocean view, we also have an archipelago to boot! Isn't it marvellous!

MAX: (*Derisively.*) That's not an archipelago.

VICTORIA: It isn't? Are you sure?

MAX: It's a field of oilrigs.

VICTORIA: No.

MAX: That "lonely cloud" is methane gas burn-off.

VICTORIA: *(Deflated.)* Oh. *(Beat.)* Oh, well that's nice too, I suppose…in its own way. Not as romantic but…not everyday either.

MAX: When did you last have your eyes tested?

(Just then another, louder, crackling of gunfire is heard.)

MAX: *(Ducking.)* Christ!

VICTORIA: Darling, that sounded awfully loud for insects, crossbred or otherwise.

MAX: That was bloody close!

VICTORIA: I seem to recall the crickets in Tunisia being rather loud – especially at night – but it all seemed rather glamorous and charming at the time. This though…well, one could almost describe it as disconcerting.

MAX: We should have stayed at home. It's this bloody climate – it breeds all kinds of monstrosities.

VICTORIA: *(As she turns to cross back to the room.)* I'd better have another pill – just to be on the safe side.

MAX: Victoria, no! I have told you I don't want your entire

experience of this–

VICTORIA: Oh, darling, don't start on again. It's not my fault – it's the way I was born, the doctor said so. I just wasn't cut out for real life – not without medication. I have a reaction to it.

MAX: You're damned well supposed to!

VICTORIA: They just take the edge off.

MAX: (*With frustration.*) Oh, then…do as you please. Drug yourself into a coma for all I care.

VICTORIA: (*Exiting.*) Shan't be a tick.

(*MAX leans over the balcony and surveys his surroundings with a disapproving scowl.*)

MAX: Christ…what a bloody shambles. Untold millions in foreign aid pumped up its arse and it still looks like a total bloody cock up. I knew this would be a disaster. (*With a sigh.*) Still, that's the price you pay for making a mistake, I suppose. And mine is spending an apologetic week in this shit hole. In retrospect I'd have been far better off keeping the old cock zipped up. It's not as if she was particularly attractive in the first place. Reminds me of a horse in some ways. Still…that said, not a bad ride. (*Pause.*) I see now why this was so cheap. A bargain getaway was promised and that's exactly what I got – and it's patently clear why. I feel like a bloody pioneer. No wonder the plane was almost empty. (*Taking a deep breath.*) Still, you're here now – more or less alone – just have to buck up and get it over with…and damn the torpedoes.

(*The sound of an explosion is heard in the distance, followed by a low rumbling. VICTORIA re-enters the balcony with a bottle of water in one hand and a small bottle of pills in the other.)*

VICTORIA: Oh no, not thunder. I'm so sick of rain. Darling, it's you – you're such a grump the bad weather follows you.

MAX: I'm surprised you can tell the difference.

VICTORIA: I wanted sun and excitement and a little exotic danger, not downpours and surly service – I can get that any day of the week in High Wycombe.

(VICTORIA takes a pill from her bottle, puts it on her tongue and washes it down with the mineral water. MAX peers skyward.)

MAX: Anyway, it's hardly likely to rain, there's not a cloud in the sky – gas emissions notwithstanding.

VICTORIA: I called downstairs again, by the way, about the cosmopolitans. They assured me they were on their way.

MAX: Bloody liars.

VICTORIA: I also asked about the crickets.

MAX: You did?

VICTORIA: He seemed to be under the impression I was referring to sports and kept referencing some West Indian team captain that I'd never heard of. So I let him finish and then patiently reiterated our annoyance with the local insect population.

MAX: Well, what in God's name do you think he can do about it?

VICTORIA: I'm not sure, but he did mention something about a skirmish happening a few streets away that was bringing fire and wrath upon the great plague of his nation, which did sound a little more reassuring – though frankly little of what he said made much sense.

MAX: Well, as long as they're taking some sort of action. I don't want to be waking up to the sound of that all night.

VICTORIA: (*Peering over the balcony.*) Darling, the small one's still there. Do you think we ought to alert someone or something?

MAX: No, no, I'm sure it's just sleeping. They do it anywhere at all times of the day in these countries.

VICTORIA: Even so, it is rather hot out. Perhaps I should sprinkle some mineral water on it.

MAX: (*Sharply.*) Leave it alone, Victoria. Don't meddle in their affairs.

(*The sound of a door being knocked from inside the room is heard.*)

VICTORIA: (*Brightly.*) Ah! That'll be the cosmopolitans.

MAX: About bloody time.

VICTORIA: (*Crossing back into the room.*) I hope they didn't make them too sweet.

MAX: (*Calling after her.*) And don't over tip! These people need to learn the rules of the game.

(*VICTORIA exits as MAX stares out ahead into the distance. Beat.*)

MAX: Good God, we serve them democracy on a plate and they

can't even rustle up a couple of cocktails without making a big bloody production of it. What a total waste of time and money. If they've no desire to better themselves and learn our ways then they should damn well out with it, cut their losses and send us on our way – with a small "thank you," if that wouldn't be asking too much. Preferably in English.

VICTORIA: (*Re-entering the balcony holding two cosmopolitans.*) Here they are! And they're just right – I cheated and took a little pre-toast sip.

MAX: (*Taking his glass.*) Let's just hope that ordering the next one will involve a little less conflict.

VICTORIA: (*Raising her glass.*) Cheers, darling!

MAX: Yes, to um…

VICTORIA: To foreign affairs. Actually, no, not to that. No, to um…

MAX: To free will!

VICTORIA: Yes! No! No, to um…

MAX: To liberty!

VICTORIA: To loyalty!

MAX: To license!

VICTORIA: To repentance!

MAX: To emancipation!

VICTORIA: To recrimination!

MAX: Oh, now you're just being idiotic. Cheers!

VICTORIA: Cheers, darling!

(*They toast their glasses and drink.*)

MAX: Mm…not bad…all things considered.

VICTORIA: They're absolutely delicious. They're even tastier than yours.

MAX: Now steady on, Victoria – don't let's get carried away simply because we're in a strange environment.

VICTORIA: (*Peering over the balcony.*) Oh, look! Some people have gathered around the small one. They've come to fetch it, by the look of it.

MAX: (*Leaning over the balcony.*) What? Where?

VICTORIA: Yes, they're wrapping it up and taking it away. Look, look, they're waving! (*With a gracious wave of her hand.*) Hello! Hello down there!

MAX: Since when do people wave with their fists clenched?

VICTORIA: Oh, don't be such an old sourpuss. It's probably customary. Wave back – show them you're pleased they're here.

MAX: I will not! That sort of gesture speaks the same in any language.

VICTORIA: Oh, you're impossible sometimes. (*Waving down with great enthusiasm.*) Hello to you! Isn't your country gorgeous! Do you think it's going to rain? (*Beat.*) Oh, they're going. What a shame. I was hoping we could strike up some sort of bi-lateral…what's it called?

MAX: Just smile and let them be – it's the best you can hope for.

VICTORIA: But I want to make a connection. I want to reach out to these people. After all, many of them share very similar characteristics to ourselves in certain ways.

MAX: And how on earth would you know that?

VICTORIA: I think I read it somewhere – or saw it on some nature programme.

> (*Another, louder, explosion is heard, followed by a loud rumbling reverberation.*)

MAX: (*Cowering slightly.*) Christ, this is ridiculous. If there's going to be an almighty storm I wish it would just hurry up and be done with. I don't think it's asking too much to be able to enjoy a quiet afternoon cocktail in peace, is it?

VICTORIA: Where are the clouds?

MAX: Clouds?

VICTORIA: If there's a storm brewing where are the clouds?

MAX: It's…I…it's thermal winds and things like that. It's all different over here, Victoria. It all sneaks up on you when you least expect it. Their entire habitat is based on treachery.

VICTORIA: Well, it must be getting close – that sounded terribly ferocious.

MAX: Yes, well…drink up and let's deal with it when it gets here.

(*They both take large swigs from their glasses.*)

VICTORIA: Incidentally, where are we eating this evening? Here in the hotel, or are we venturing into town?

MAX: In the hotel, of course. We can't just waltz into the streets in some blasé manner without an escort.

VICTORIA: Why would we need an escort?

(*Just then another, extremely loud, burst of gunfire is heard. MAX drops his glass and fall to the floor.*)

MAX: Jesus bloody Christ!

VICTORIA: (*Seemingly oblivious.*) I mean, we don't need escorting around High Wycombe. Why so here?

MAX: (*Pulling himself up, sounding frantic.*) This place is a madhouse!

VICTORIA: (*Distractedly.*) It is a little unusual, isn't it?

MAX: I can't take it, Victoria! I can't take any more of it! It's too much – even for me. And now my bloody drink's gone! (*Spotting her pill bottle.*) Give me those!

VICTORIA: What?

MAX: Those pills! I'm up to here with this place! I need something else. I've tried – bloody valiantly, I would say – but that's it! I'm only a man – I'm only human. Hand them over!

VICTORIA: Oh, darling, you've no idea how delighted I am to hear you say that. Here... (*Offering the pill bottle.*) Take as many as you wish.

(*MAX takes the pill bottle, empties a handful of pills into his hand, grabs VICTORIA'S drink and swills them down.*)

VICTORIA: Oh, Max, you look just like a child. A sweet, frightened child. It's really quite touching. You know, I...I never expected this little holiday to bring us closer together – especially under the conditions in which it was assembled – but...well, I think it has, hasn't it? Albeit in a somewhat rough-hewn manner.

MAX: Hmm?

VICTORIA: Perhaps this was our destiny. Perhaps after all that pain...conflict...deceit...this was all somehow...I don't know...inevitable. It's a nice thought, at least.

MAX: (*Finishing the rest of her drink, the pills already beginning to take effect.*) I understand what you're saying...Victoria...but I...I don't know that I fully comprehend the meaning of your words...or, that is to say...something similar...or words to that effect.

VICTORIA: I know, darling, you don't have to explain.

MAX: It's just that it's all so...I don't know...there.

VICTORIA: Absolutely it is...and why not, I say?

MAX: Yes, why not? To hell with the lot of them!

(Just then another burst of very loud, very close, gunfire is heard. VICTORIA nonchalantly takes the pill bottle from MAX, takes out another pill and pops it in her mouth.)

MAX: And if it all gets a bit…or…or spat at, then…then that's just the price one pays.

VICTORIA: My thoughts exactly – well said, darling.

MAX: Balls to it all – and up the arse, too! And, anyway, we'll be home in a few days.

VICTORIA: Oh, don't say that. You'll get me all depressed.

MAX: Why not? It's true.

VICTORIA: I know, but I want to enjoy this, nonetheless.

MAX: What on earth for? What's to enjoy?

VICTORIA: I don't know, the whole…tribalistic…earthy… internationalism of it all. And because it's a little escape and I need it.

MAX: Yes, escape. Let's escape. Where shall we go?

VICTORIA: Darling, we're already here.

MAX: Where?

VICTORIA: Here. This is it. This is our escape.

MAX: Yes, of course it is – and very nice, too.

VICTORIA: *(Peering over the balcony, her voice animated.)* Oh!

MAX: (*In singsong fashion.*) Oh, oh, oh!

VICTORIA: Max, look! Look it's a carnival of some description! Or perhaps they're travelling players – it's hard to tell.

MAX: Oh, I do so love a carnival. I think I'm starting to get in the mood. Let the band play on!

> (*Just then another loud explosion is heard, followed by an intense, thunderous rumble.*)

VICTORIA: And look, and they have a little donkey – with a little cart attached.

MAX: (*Looking over the balcony.*) Charming…utterly charming.

VICTORIA: Do you think they're going to play something for us?

MAX: Play what?

VICTORIA: I don't know – some sort of local medley.

MAX: Yes, yes I'm sure they'll strike up something.

VICTORIA: Oh, how wonderful! Perhaps I should order more drinks?

MAX: Excellent idea.

> (*VICTORIA darts back into the room as MAX leans over the balcony and shouts down to the new arrivals.*)

MAX: Afternoon to you! Would you by any chance be familiar with a rather enchanting little tune entitled, "Lady in Red"? (*Beat.*) Beg pardon? Didn't quite catch that. (*Beat.*) That neither, but never mind. Just toss out what you have…whatever's in your repertoire…something catchy, preferably.

(*VICTORIA re-emerges from the room, looking somewhat perturbed.*)

VICTORIA: Darling, the phone's dead…there's just nothing there. I don't wish to complain, but these are basic human services and I think you ought to speak to someone about it.

MAX: Don't get so het up, Victoria, you're on holiday. And besides, the travelling minstrels are about to start up. I asked for Chris DeBurgh, but I don't think it translated.

VICTORIA: Oh, what a shame! So what are they going to play?

MAX: I have no idea. I thought I heard one of them say "Allahu Akbar," but I couldn't tell you if that was the name of the song or the artiste – I'm not even sure if I'm being phonetically correct.

VICTORIA: Oh, what's the difference? It'll set the mood, in any case.

MAX: Let's hope so.

(*Pause.*)

VICTORIA: Thank you for this, Max.

MAX: For what?

VICTORIA: This. You may be tired of me but you still cared enough to do this.

MAX: Oh, shut up, old girl – you know I'd be lost without you.

VICTORIA: Would you?

MAX: Of course I would. (*Beat.*) Besides, divorce is not only a quitter's game, it's also something that – under current fiscal conditions – is completely off the table.

VICTORIA: Darling, how sweet! (*Looking back over the balcony.*) Oh, look! Look!

MAX: What is it?

VICTORIA: They've opened up the little cart. It looks like they're about to set off some fireworks.

MAX: (*Leaning over the balcony.*) Now? Why now, for heaven's sake?

VICTORIA: Don't question it, darling, just enjoy the spectacle.

MAX: But it's daylight. I want to see the bright lights. I want bang and flash.

VICTORIA: Well, perhaps you will, but in a novel way. They have a different slant on things over here – who knows what they'll send up for us?

MAX: Do you think they have any Roman Candles?

VICTORIA: (*Excitedly.*) Oh, look! I think they're about to fire off the rockets!

MAX: (*Putting his arm around her shoulder.*) Bravo! Smile and wave, darling – it'll mean the world to them.

(MAX and VICTORIA smile and wave down to the assembly below. MAX'S smile soon turns into a frown.)

MAX: *(With some concern.)* Wait a minute – should they be pointed at quite that angle?

VICTORIA: What?

MAX: The rockets.

VICTORIA: *(With increasing excitement.)* Yes, yes, I'm sure they should! Oh, how thrilling this is!

MAX: But look, they're pointed–

VICTORIA: Just enjoy the show, Max – I'm sure they know exactly what they're doing! *(Ecstatically.)* Oh God, it's all so madly foreign! I feel like I'm in heaven!

MAX: But won't they–

VICTORIA: Oh, look, look! They're off! Here we go!

(As MAX and VICTORIA continue waving – MAX frowning, VICTORIA smiling – the stage is suddenly engulfed in blazing white light as the sound of a deafening explosion reverberates throughout the auditorium. BLACKOUT.)

END OF PLAY

ABOUT THE AUTHOR

From the Royal Court Theatre in London to the Playhouse Theatre in Tasmania, the works of award-winning playwright Andrew Biss have been performed across the globe, spanning four continents. His plays have won awards on both coasts of the U.S., critical acclaim in the U.K., and quickly became a perennial sight on Off and Off-Off Broadway stages.

In London his plays have been performed at The Royal Court Theatre, Theatre503, Riverside Studios, The Pleasance Theatre, The Union Theatre, The White Bear Theatre, The Brockley Jack Studio Theatre, Fractured Lines Theatre & Film at COG ARTSpace, and Ghost Dog Productions at The Horse & Stables.

In New York his plays have been produced at Theatre Row Studios, The Samuel French Off-Off-Broadway Festival, The Kraine Theater, The Red Room Theater, Times Square Arts Center, Manhattan Theatre Source, Mind The Gap Theatre, 3Graces Theatre Company, Emerging Artists Theatre, Curan Repertory Company, Pulse Ensemble Theatre, American Globe Theatre, The American Theater of Actors, and Chashama Theatres, among others.

His plays and monologues are published in numerous anthologies from trade publishers Bedford/St. Martin's, Smith & Kraus, Inc., Pioneer Drama Service, and Applause Theatre & Cinema Books.

Andrew is a graduate of the University of the Arts London, and a member of the Dramatists Guild of America, Inc.

For more information please visit his website at:
www.andrewbiss.com.

The End of the World

5M/3F Approx. 90 minutes

Valentine's parents have decided that the time has finally come for their son to leave home and discover life for himself. As he ventures forth into the vast world beyond, his new adventure is soon drawn to a halt when he is mugged at gunpoint. Frightened and exhausted, he seeks shelter at a bed and breakfast establishment named The End of the World, run by the dour Mrs. Anna. Here Valentine encounters a Bosnian woman with a hole where her stomach used to be, an American entrepreneur with a scheme to implant televisions into people's foreheads, and a Catholic priest who attempts to lure him down inside a kitchen sink. Then things start getting strange...

In this story based loosely around the state of Bardo from The Tibetan Book of the Dead - an intermediate state where the dead arrive prior to rebirth - dying is the easy part. Getting out of Bardo and returning to the land of the living is a far more perilous proposition, and unless you know what you're doing...you might never leave.

An odd, yet oddly touching tale of life, death, and the space in-between.

Leah's Gals

3M/5F Approx. 90 minutes

Leah's just won the lottery in what she describes as "the biggest single, one-time cash haul in this here dirt-poor, shitty state's history!" But, rather than living the highlife, Leah decides to split the winnings among her three daughters, asking only for a deathbed-style declaration of love in return. When her youngest daughter, Patina, scoffs at the idea, Leah disowns her with vitriolic fury. Bestowing instead the prize money upon her two eldest daughters, her dreams of a pampered retirement in the arms of her offspring for herself and her close companion, Pearl, seem guaranteed. Things soon turn sour, however, as long-held grievances and newfound wealth lead to familial treachery, violence and death.

Greed, lust, drugs, and Capodimonte combust in this low-rent, Southern fried twist on a literary classic.

The Meta Plays

A collection of short comedic plays that take theatrical conventions on a metaphysical joyride.

This unique compilation of wittily inventive short comedies can be performed by as few as 4 actors or as many as 18, all with minimal set and prop requirements. Many of these plays have gone on to receive highly successful productions around the world, garnering glowing reviews along the way.

Arcane Acts of Urban Renewal

Five One-Act Comedies Approx. 100 minutes

A collection of five thematically related, darkly humorous one-act plays in which ordinary people find themselves in the most extraordinary circumstances.

An Honest Mistake: Madge has long since surrendered herself to the verbal abuse doled out to her by her belligerent husband, Stan. On this particular evening, however, her fears of a rat beneath the floorboards, combined with her absent-mindedness, result in her dishing up Stan not only his evening meal - but also his just deserts!

A Familiar Face: Two elderly women, old friends, meet up in a London café shortly after one them – Dora – has been widowed. As Dora's grief and anger intensifies, her good friend Eydie begins to suspect there may be more to her angst than the loss of a loved one. When Dora calmly removes from her shopping bag a large glass jar containing a human head, discussions over its mysterious identity, and how it came to be lodged in the cupboard under her stairs, lead to some startling revelations.

A Slip of the Tongue: Miss Perkins, tired of the constant innuendos and sexual insinuations of her employer, Mr. Reams, has decided to hand in her notice. On this particular morning, however, Mr. Reams decides to take things one step further. Unfortunately, due to Miss Perkins' nervous disposition and a telephone that rings at a disturbingly high pitch, he soon discovers he's bitten off more than he can chew...or at least, one of them has.

An Embarrassing Odour: Ethel, a widowed pensioner, sits down one evening to tackle her daily crossword puzzle. Suddenly her tranquil world is turned upside down when a burglar enters her home, believing it to be unoccupied. As Ethel vainly attempts to forge a relationship with the violent delinquent before her, his concerns lie only with getting his hands on her valuables...that and the unpleasant smell that fills the room. What is that smell?

A Stunning Confession: During an evening in front of the television a staid married couple suddenly find themselves having to confront a new reality.

Suburban Redux

3M/1F or 2M/2F Approx. 90 minutes

After thirty years of arid matrimony and suburban monotony, Mrs. Pennington-South's only dream was that her son, Cuthbert, would break free of the cycle of upper-middle class inertia that had suffocated her. Raising him in the hope that he was homosexual, she soon begins dragging home potential suitors for tea – on this particular occasion a rather shy, awkward young man named Tristram. Cuthbert, however, finds he can no longer maintain his façade and at last confesses to his mother his guilty secret: his heterosexuality.

When Cuthbert leaves to meet Trixie, his new female friend, Mrs. Pennington-South – heartbroken but accepting – takes solace in the company of Tristram, and a mutual love of the arts soon leads to a new found friendship. After several weeks, however, Tristram's feelings take on more amorous overtones, and a confession of love for a woman almost thirty years his senior sends Mrs. Pennington-South into a state of emotional turmoil. Her anxiety is further heightened by the unexpected arrival of Cuthbert, merrily announcing that he has brought Trixie home for an introduction, and of the "big news" they wish to impart.

Mrs. Pennington-South, mortified at having to face the reality of her son's lifestyle choice, fearfully awaits the dreaded Trixie. Nothing, however, could have prepared her for what would come next.

A Ballyhoo in Blighty

The multi-award winning, critically acclaimed "Indigenous Peoples" (Winner "Best Play" – New York's Wonderland One-Act Festival) is paired with three other cheeky, uproarious comedies in what is guaranteed to be an unforgettable, side-splitting evening's entertainment.

Also included are "The Man Who Liked Dick", "Kitchen Sink Drama" and "Carbon-Based Life Form Seeks Similar" – all outrageously funny British comedies that have received lauded productions in London, New York and beyond.

Cast size: 4M / 5F (Roles can be doubled for a 2M/2F cast configuration)

Made in the USA
Columbia, SC
14 July 2019